Foreword

Welcome to the ISTE Standards for Students, your road map to transforming learning and teaching alongside today's connected learners.

These standards are designed to empower students to be owners of the learning process and ensure that learning is a blend of exploration, creativity and discovery. They are about meeting the needs of learners who live, work and play in a globally connected world.

Empowered Learner. Digital Citizen. Knowledge Constructor. Innovative Designer. Computational Thinker. Creative Communicator. Global Collaborator.

The names of the standards point to both the functional and aspirational roles of today's learners.

In this guide, you'll find definitions of each standard along with scenarios for authentic learning activities that build students' essential skills, a crosswalk comparing these standards to previous iterations, and a prerequisite foundational technology skills scope and sequence document – all designed to show you what the Student Standards look like in practice.

I want to express my sincere appreciation to the thousands of educators and hundreds of students who contributed to the Student Standards. Their input was invaluable in the creation of these exciting standards that are giving a voice to learners around the world.

> Richard Culatta
> ISTE CEO

Using this booklet

This booklet is your guide to the refreshed standards. The standards are presented amid content that defines and characterizes them and answers the important question, what do the ISTE Standards for Students look like in practice? In the following sections you will find:

- The ISTE Standards for Students.
- Nine scenarios describing authentic learning activities that build Student Standards skills.
- Skills by age band for what can be expected to support design of learning activities.
- A crosswalk comparing the ISTE Standards for Students (2016) to the ISTE Standards for Students (2007).
- A prerequisite foundational technology skills scope and sequence table.

Preface

The ISTE Standards are about learning, not tools. They reflect and further a shared goal to bring deep, transformative learning to our students. They were developed for educators by educators. Practitioners use them to guide empowered student learning, and leaders rely on them to advance an innovative vision for learning with technology.

Make the standards work for you

- If you're an educator, use the standards to guide your learning design, inspire your professional growth and advocate for dynamic learning in your school. You can find support and resources at iste.org/standardsforstudents.

- If you're an education leader, use the standards to guide your vision and goals around digital learning and teaching, using them to support systemwide plans – including professional growth, school improvement and technology plans as well as curriculum mapping – or in your LMS or web system. A decision to use in any one of these ways is considered an adoption by ISTE. To help you on your way, access the free report, "Redefining learning in a technology-driven world: A report to support adoption of the ISTE Standards for Students" at iste.org/StandardsReport.

Help ISTE support you

- Educators can download the standards using the permissions process, which contributes to rich data that ISTE uses when designing resources and making the case for the standards. With permissions, you also receive a PDF of the standards, a toolkit to support your use and other resources as they become available.

- Leaders, share your story. Let ISTE know about your decision to adopt the standards so we can support your efforts, measure the impact of the standards and share your success. Take this short survey at iste.org/StandardsSurvey.

Questions, ideas or suggestions? Share them with standards@iste.org.

Contents

Realizing the Promise of Technology

Since the first desktop computers were installed in a classroom or computer lab, educators have experienced cognitive dissonance regarding how to best use that technology to support student learning. On one hand, teachers and administrators suggest that technology has the potential to transform student learning. And yet, more often than not, we see technology used primarily to automate marginally effective traditional instructional strategies. We know the latter does not impact student learning, but we continue to promote low-level, ineffective uses for classroom technology. It's well past time to move beyond rudimentary use of classroom technology. A December 2015 report from the Organisation for Economic Co-Operation and Development finds that schools still are not taking advantage of technology's potential to ameliorate the impact of the digital divide and level the instructional playing field. But things don't have to be this way. We have access to technologies that were the stuff of science fiction less than a decade ago. We have research that points out pathways to making differences in student learning. And now we have the ISTE Standards for Students that lead with learning by focusing on encouraging students to engage in deeper learning – to take ownership of their learning, becoming more effective learners in and outside the classroom.

Standards as a Fulcrum of Change

One definition for fulcrum is the point on which a lever rests. Another definition that is more germane for this discussion is "Something that plays an indispensible role in an activity or situation." How does this pertain to the ISTE Standards?

Education institutions have changed in the last 30-plus years. Perhaps not to the degree some of us would like to see, but there are differences. More schools than ever have broadband connectivity. Most schools have developed policies related to classroom use of technology. The ratio of students to internet-connected devices continues to decrease. We're poised to make significant change, but need something to give us the buy-in required to move in the right direction. That something is the ISTE Standards for Students – the fulcrum educators can use to apply leverage for change.

Emily Dickinson said, "I dwell in possibility." In revising the Student Standards, ISTE's goal was not only to reflect what is possible in terms of instructional technology, but also to anticipate how pedagogy could be changed and improved in the future through the use of technology. This means keeping in mind that in order to serve today's kindergartener, it was imperative to develop standards that will have a shelf life that will take her through most of her academic career. This focus on the future is designed to help ISTE keep things real while remembering to always consider the possibilities.

Underlying Assumptions

When the original standards were developed in 1998, it was assumed that the primary focus for student learning needed to be on how to use technology tools. By 2007, when the standards were refreshed the first time, this underlying assumption had changed. Emphasis shifted to the importance of cognitive and learning skills, along with creativity and innovation. But basic skills were still the focal point of one standard. Now, with this latest standards refresh, underlying assumptions have changed once again. In this new iteration of the standards, the focus is squarely on learning, not tools. Yes, students still need to be proficient in foundational technology skills, but that's not the end. It's the means to an end where the expectation is that students will use technology when appropriate to take charge of their own learning.

There are additional underlying assumptions that informed the work of developing these refreshed standards. For example, the committee wanted to ensure that these standards would work for students of all ages in concert with content area standards, but also be able to stand alone when necessary. It was important that the performance indicators describe behavior that is measurable or observable, but at the same time make it clear it is not ISTE's intention that these standards be used to lay the foundation for high-stakes standardized testing of students' technology proficiency. Finally, the standards are vendor and technology neutral. The reasoning is that by emphasizing learning over specific tools, the standards can be relevant for the next five to 10 years, giving students and teachers ample time to become familiar with them.

Themes and Shifts in the Standards

If they aren't based on themes promoting students "using" technology, what is the thrust of the ISTE Standards for Students? The new standards provide an aspirational framework to leverage technology for learning transformation by:

- Capitalizing on recognized attributes of responsible learners.
- Offering increased opportunities for learner-driven activities.
- Serving academic and workforce goals.
- Clearly aligning with content area standards in both language and goals.
- Including the learning sciences in relationship to pedagogy and learning environments.

Themes interwoven throughout the standards also reflect shifts in thinking about how technology can be leveraged to transform learning and are critical to include in conversations about the new standards. They include:

- Empowered learning, which includes motivating students to engage more fully in their education by allowing them to make choices about their learning and encouraging self-reliance.
- The evolution of our thinking about where the locus of control lies in modern learning environments (from teacher-directed to student-centered to learner-driven) and how that impacts new ideas about education.
- The emergence of new key roles for teachers. For example, there was an assumption that when given the freedom to pursue their own interests, students would leap at the chance to be more self-directed. In reality, most students need more guidance than anticipated as they to learn to take more responsibility for their own learning. Teachers are the logical people to offer this critical support.
- The emergence of new roles for students. Teachers can assist students in accepting new roles by preparing students for greater autonomy, but students also need to rise to the challenge if they are to become empowered learners.
- The identification of how learning can change when technology is leveraged for authentic, purposeful activities and deeper, engaged learning.

Refreshing the standards is serious business. ISTE has reached out to stakeholders around the world to engage in a process meant to result in a shared vision of what becomes possible when technology is used appropriately in education settings. But the real work begins once the standards are released. If the refreshed standards go no further than national, state or provincial levels, there will be no impact on what happens in classrooms. Local educators – teachers, principals and heads of schools, as well as those who support site staff – must work to understand the standards and implement them. Innovative education organizations will invest in curriculum development, adopting new instructional strategies and professional development. Let's begin!

ISTE Standards for Students

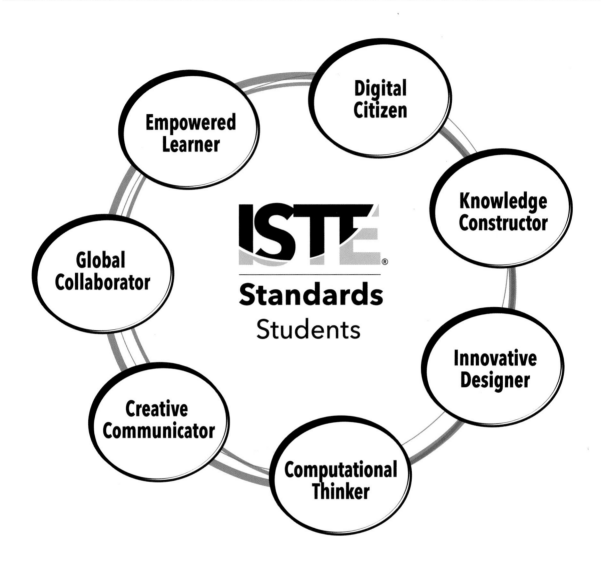

The Student Standards emphasize the skills and qualities we want for students, enabling them to engage and thrive in a connected, digital world. The standards are designed for use by educators across the curriculum with every age student, with a goal of cultivating these skills throughout a student's academic career. Both students and teachers will be responsible for achieving foundational technology skills to fully apply the standards. The reward, however, will be educators who skillfully mentor and inspire students to amplify learning with technology, and challenge them to be agents of their own learning.

1. Empowered Learner

Students leverage technology to take an active role in choosing, achieving and demonstrating competency in their learning goals, informed by the learning sciences. Students:

a. Articulate and set personal learning goals, develop strategies leveraging technology to achieve them and reflect on the learning process itself to improve learning outcomes.
b. Build networks and customize their learning environments in ways that support the learning process.
c. Use technology to seek feedback that informs and improves their practice and to demonstrate their learning in a variety of ways.
d. Understand the fundamental concepts of technology operations, demonstrate the ability to choose, use and troubleshoot current technologies and are able to transfer their knowledge to explore emerging technologies.

2. Digital Citizen

Students recognize the rights, responsibilities and opportunities of living, learning and working in an interconnected digital world, and they act and model in ways that are safe, legal and ethical. Students:

a. Cultivate and manage their digital identity and reputation and are aware of the permanence of their actions in the digital world.
b. Engage in positive, safe, legal and ethical behavior when using technology, including social interactions online or when using networked devices.
c. Demonstrate an understanding of and respect for the rights and obligations of using and sharing intellectual property.
d. Manage their personal data to maintain digital privacy and security and are aware of data-collection technology used to track their navigation online.

3. Knowledge Constructor

Students critically curate a variety of resources using digital tools to construct knowledge, produce creative artifacts and make meaningful learning experiences for themselves and others. Students:

a. Plan and employ effective research strategies to locate information and other resources for their intellectual or creative pursuits.
b. Evaluate the accuracy, perspective, credibility and relevance of information, media, data or other resources.
c. Curate information from digital resources using a variety of tools and methods to create collections of artifacts that demonstrate meaningful connections or conclusions.
d. Build knowledge by actively exploring real-world issues and problems, developing ideas and theories and pursuing answers and solutions.

4. Innovative Designer

Students use a variety of technologies within a design process to identify and solve problems by creating new, useful or imaginative solutions. Students:

a. Know and use a deliberate design process for generating ideas, testing theories, creating innovative artifacts or solving authentic problems.
b. Select and use digital tools to plan and manage a design process that considers design constraints and calculated risks.
c. Develop, test and refine prototypes as part of a cyclical design process.
d. Exhibit a tolerance for ambiguity, perseverance and the capacity to work with open-ended problems.

5. Computational Thinker

Students develop and employ strategies for understanding and solving problems in ways that leverage the power of technological methods to develop and test solutions. Students:

a. Formulate problem definitions suited for technology-assisted methods such as data analysis, abstract models and algorithmic thinking in exploring and finding solutions.
b. Collect data or identify relevant data sets, use digital tools to analyze them, and represent data in various ways to facilitate problem-solving and decision-making.
c. Break problems into component parts, extract key information, and develop descriptive models to understand complex systems or facilitate problem-solving.
d. Understand how automation works and use algorithmic thinking to develop a sequence of steps to create and test automated solutions.

6. Creative Communicator

Students communicate clearly and express themselves creatively for a variety of purposes using the platforms, tools, styles, formats and digital media appropriate to their goals. Students:

a. Choose the appropriate platforms and tools for meeting the desired objectives of their creation or communication.
b. Create original works or responsibly repurpose or remix digital resources into new creations.
c. Communicate complex ideas clearly and effectively by creating or using a variety of digital objects such as visualizations, models or simulations.
d. Publish or present content that customizes the message and medium for their intended audiences.

7. Global Collaborator

Students use digital tools to broaden their perspectives and enrich their learning by collaborating with others and working effectively in teams locally and globally. Students:

a. Use digital tools to connect with learners from a variety of backgrounds and cultures, engaging with them in ways that broaden mutual understanding and learning.
b. Use collaborative technologies to work with others, including peers, experts or community members, to examine issues and problems from multiple viewpoints.
c. Contribute constructively to project teams, assuming various roles and responsibilities to work effectively toward a common goal.
d. Explore local and global issues and use collaborative technologies to work with others to investigate solutions.

Scenarios

The following section provides examples of what the ISTE Standards for Students look like in the classroom. Nine scenarios describe, by age band, authentic activities that reflect not only Student Standards, but also relevant curriculum standards, underscoring an ISTE core belief that technology use should not occur in isolation but as an integral part of learning across all skills and subject areas. The scenarios – informed by conversations with instructional technology experts and educators from around the world – depict real examples and promising practices from around the globe.

Thanks to following educators for sharing their valuable ideas and expertise:

- Zephonia Avant, early childhood curriculum specialist, South Central Service Cooperative, Camden, Arkansas

- Kathy Dorr, professional development specialist, Northwest Council for Computer Education, Bellingham, Washington

- Sarah Carpenter, digital learning coach, American School, Seoul Foreign School, Seoul, Republic of Korea

- Tara Linney, edtech coach, Singapore American School, Singapore

- Kevin Jarrett, teacher, Northfield Community Middle School, Northfield, New Jersey

- Bob Garguilo, teacher, Northfield Community Middle School, Northfield, New Jersey

- Glenn Robbins, principal, Northfield Community Middle School, Northfield, New Jersey

- Cheryl Rose, STEAM teacher, Desert Mirage Elementary School, Glendale, Arizona

- Shelly Luke Wille, head of school, Chadwick International School, Incheon, Republic of Korea

- Mahmud Shihab, director of the Educational Resources Center and head of educational technology, International College, Beirut, Lebanon

Scenarios for Ages 4-7

Scenario 1
Programming with Robots

Four- and 5-year-old students hone math and problem-solving skills using programmable devices.

Age Level: 4- and 5-year-olds
Content Area: Mathematics

Learning Environment: One robot and one, 3' x 3' mat (6-inch grid) per classroom, free-choice learning center
Technology: Programmable toy robots

Students ages 4 and 5 learn basics that lay the foundation for skills they will use throughout their lifetimes in academics, critical thinking and problem-solving. These skills include sequencing, estimation, counting, one-to-one correspondence, spatial relationships, cause and effect and more.

Teachers in the program described here have explored and implemented the appropriate use of technology in their classrooms for several years. They have learned that, with thoughtful planning, various mobile devices can be used to enhance learning – even with 4- to 5-year-olds. Recently, the legislature in the state where these teachers work passed a comprehensive law requiring that all public and charter high schools offer coding classes. It wasn't long before the teachers started hearing about coding experiences for younger children that involved the use of programmable devices. The curriculum incorporates opportunities for children to learn through play, and there are times when they are given free choice of activities. Building in use of simple robots appealed to teachers as a logical way to allow children to hone important skills in an exploratory environment.

Typically, toy robots move forward or backward (6 inches at a time), and rotate 90 degrees left or right. They are programmed by pressing buttons on top of the robot. So, to move the robot forward 12 inches and then turn around and go back to where it started, a child would press the forward button two times, press either the right or left turn button two times, and then press the forward button two times – a sequence of six directions. Toy robots can accept a predetermined number of commands, and some offer accessories such as floor mats of various sizes with 6-inch grids. Students use these mats to complete programming tasks like moving the robot from one location on the grid to another using a series of commands. The teachers began by providing challenges for students to complete.

Once they are comfortable using the mat as an aid to estimating distances, the children program the robots to navigate paths and mazes they've constructed using building blocks, resulting in a mix of teacher-created and student-designed activities. The children's ideas are typically spontaneous, arising out of their play. Given a flexible working environment and freedom to develop their own challenges, use of programmable toy robots is very powerful. Recently, two of the children and their teachers attended a conference where the students demonstrated their programming skills to educators from around their state.

What is the connection to the Student Standards?

Empowered Learner – Students in these preschool classrooms are making choices about which learning goals they want to explore and how they want to proceed. Their use of programmable toy robots is based on free choice during center time, and they can choose between using teacher-created programming challenges or creating their own.

Knowledge Constructor – As these young students move from teacher-created activities to devising programming experiments of their own, they are developing ideas and theories about how to complete a challenge and then pursuing answers and solutions by trying various programming strategies.

Innovative Designer – One attribute of innovative designers is perseverance, a willingness to stick with a problem until a solution is found. The preschoolers demonstrate perseverance as they work to complete each challenge.

Computational Thinker – In the process of identifying a sequence of steps that will complete a challenge, students are collecting and analyzing data as they explore possible solutions.

Scenarios for Ages 4-7

Scenario 2
Biomes and Habitats

In this scenario, 7-year-old students prepare team projects they will use to teach classmates about biomes and habitats.

Age Level: 7-year-olds
Content Area: Science, language arts, geography

Learning Environment: Four laptops and four tablets per classroom
Technology: Computers and tablets

Students often get their first introduction to biomes and habitats at age 7. Children are typically fascinated with science at this age, but the vocabulary and breadth of the content can be overwhelming. Rather than expect each child to conduct an in-depth study of every biome included in the unit, a pair of primary teachers decided to approach this science unit in a different way.

They began by providing a brief overview of biomes to the entire class. This included an explanation of what biomes are and an introduction to the seven biomes they would be studying. Then their approach took a new turn. Understanding that even children this young prefer activities where they are creating something as opposed to memorizing basic information, the teachers asked their young charges to: work in trios to conduct online research about one of the seven biomes; select a project idea from a list of suggestions; design and create their chosen project; and use that project to teach the rest of the class about their assigned biome.

Primary students typically need more instructional support than older elementary and secondary students. This entails more teacher planning time, but the children's need for additional scaffolding does not preclude their abilities to take initiative, work collaboratively, think critically and demonstrate their learning through technology-supported learning activities. What does planning and implementation look like?

First, students needed a workspace for accessing links to digital research materials easy enough for them to use. The teachers opted to use an online curation tool they'd used with students previously to create an interactive Biomes & Habitats lesson. Students in each classroom had access to four tablets and four laptops. These devices were used to create or document the final student projects. Teachers also created a class workspace so students could easily turn in digital assignments. Since students were already familiar with these tools, no time was required to teach basic technology skills.

The online lesson included four questions each student team answered related to its biome. The questions ranged from basic comprehension to analyzing information that was presented in the online lesson. Students took notes digitally or using paper and pencil, making note of sources they'd used so they could cite these when they created their projects. Once they responded to the questions, student teams chose a project idea from a list provided at the end of the online activity. They were also permitted to pitch an original project idea to their teacher. Project suggestions included tasks like recording a podcast, writing an ebook and making diagrams or models. Technology tools were available, but not necessarily required.

As each team completed its project, one member turned in either the project itself or detailed photos of the project. On the final day of this unit, each team taught the rest of the class about the biome they studied, using their project as an instructional aid. Finally, student projects were posted online for ongoing reference.

What is the connection to the ISTE Standards for Students?

Empowered Learner – The 7-year-olds are asked to either choose from a list of ideas for their projects or pitch an original idea to their teacher. This approach enables them to take responsibility for their learning and demonstrate that learning in a variety of ways.

Digital Citizen – By noting and citing sources, students are learning to abide with copyright and fair use laws.

Knowledge Constructor – With support from their teachers, these youngsters are learning to locate and evaluate information related to learning topics. The project requirement ensures students create one or more artifacts related to their learning.

Creative Communicator – In the course of teaching peers about a biome, students are afforded opportunities to present knowledge based on information they have customized for a specific audience.

Global Collaborator – As they complete their team projects, students are working collaboratively and contributing constructively to produce products they can share with classmates and learners from other backgrounds.

Scenarios for Ages 8-11

Scenario 1
Newton's Laws of Motion

Nine- and 10-year-old students increase writing and speaking skills as they demonstrate their understanding of Newton's Laws of Motion.

Age Level: 9- to 10-year-olds
Content Area: Physical science, language arts, video production

Learning Environment: 1:1 laptops, tablets
Technology: Any device that can record video (digital camera, tablet, smartphone, etc.), laptops

It's one thing to rattle off one of Newton's Laws of Motion such as, "An object in motion stays in motion and an object at rest stays at rest unless they are acted upon by an outside force." It's quite another thing to really understand what the laws mean, explain one and be able to cite original real-world examples – particularly if you are 8 or 9 years old. But that's exactly what a group of elementary students have done.

The students were provided instruction and engaged in hands-on explorations in an instructional unit that covered forces and motion. As they worked through each part of the unit, students were provided ample time to grasp the content. The culminating activity for the unit was for students to work in three-person teams to make a 3- to 5-minute video explaining their choice of one of the three laws of motion. Each video was required to include an explanation of the concept, an experiment to illustrate the law and a demonstration of a real-world example of the law.

Teachers in this school are committed to regularly offering students opportunities to use various technologies for creating original products to demonstrate their understanding of complex concepts presented in class. In the process of doing this, skills from additional content areas are incorporated into activities, as appropriate. In this example, skills in language arts and video production were used to help students demonstrate their learning of concepts in physical science. As a result, between seven and eight hours of additional class time was devoted to recording and producing the videos. Skills covered included writing a script, creating a detailed online storyboard, and shooting and editing the video. Students were also responsible for completing pre-production tasks such as gathering props and materials for experiments, finding a suitable location for shooting, and scheduling and conducting rehearsals. All students had laptop computers which they used to research their topics, work collaboratively on scripts and create their storyboards. Each team had access to tablet devices to shoot and edit their videos.

The initial audience for their work is the teachers who use the videos to assess students' understanding of the content. However, once assessed for accuracy, videos that met the required criteria were posted online in a project blog for use by other teachers and students as tools for learning, and for viewing by family members and friends.

What is the connection to the Student Standards?

Empowered Learner – Although teachers select the type of technology that is used for this activity, students are making the videos to create artifacts that demonstrate their learning.

Knowledge Constructor – Students use multiple sources for the research conducted prior to developing a script, including online materials, which helps them expand their understanding of the material they will present in the video.

Creative Communicator – The project requirements for sharing experiments and including demonstrations as content is developed to document their understanding of concepts presented during the instructional unit helps students become more creative communicators.

Scenarios for Ages 8-11

Scenario 2
Solving Real-World Community Problems

Ten and 11-year old students design tools to help community members cope during heavy winter storms.

Age Level: 10- to 11-year-olds
Content Area: Science, social studies

Learning Environment: Makerspace classroom
Technology: Laptops, tablets, digital cameras, electronic building blocks

When a recent winter storm dumped 2 feet of snow overnight, fifth grade students at one middle school used the storm to provide context for their upcoming design project on weather. Students personalized the five-day activity by focusing on identifying ways they could make their neighbors' lives easier or better during the next large storm event.

Students began by self-selecting two- and three-person teams, then brainstorming ways they could help or protect people and animals in the next storm. They also took a look at ways to enjoy themselves during a snowstorm. This led to lists of things students could create that could be helpful or just plain fun. Ideas included items such as modified snow shovels, a collapsible tarp for temporary covered parking, thermal boots, a hot cocoa cozy, a flying sled and a snowball launcher. A popular idea was a rock salt blower designed to make it easy for senior citizens to salt their sidewalks. While creative ideas abounded, the class instructor reports it would have been helpful to take additional time to delve even more deeply into the process of identifying real needs and possible solutions.

With just five days for the entire project, teams took their ideas and started working on prototypes. The learning environment was a makerspace classroom, so there were many tools and materials to choose from ranging from high-tech to no-tech. Aside from a need for better tools for cutting things like Styrofoam, the teams were able to fabricate their prototypes using items available in the classroom. Once prototypes were constructed, a video was made of each team as they explained the need they identified and how their product provided a solution.

In reflecting on the experience, the instructor identified three modifications he will make in the future. First, he will provide less direct instruction to give students more time to build and create. Second, he will have even more supplies and additional tools on hand. And finally, teams will be responsible for creating a design brief using an online presentation program.

What is the connection to the Student Standards?

Empowered Learner – While the challenge is designed by the teacher, student teams have a great deal of autonomy when it comes to determining how they will solve the problem posed. They are also able to continue the project into the next school year.

Digital Citizen – Design challenges are an appropriate venue for teaching students about intellectual property in terms of their own designs and when looking for ideas in designs created by others.

Knowledge Constructor – Research is a critical piece in design challenges in conducting needs analyses and in product development.

Innovative Designer – The entire project is based on students using a design process to identify and solve problems by creating new, useful or imaginative solutions.

Creative Communicator – The project requirements for teams to explain their prototypes and how these meet a specific need help them become more creative communicators.

Global Collaborator – In the course of developing a more empathetic approach to problem-solving, students learn to view a challenge from a perspective other than their own. For example, students think about problems related to major winter storms from the point of view of a senior citizen or a parent with young children.

Scenarios for Ages 8-11

Scenario 3
We're All Immigrants

During a study of immigration, two classes of 10 and 11-year old students located on different continents collaborate to gather and share data about their families' histories, helping them gain a better understanding of this timely topic.

Age Level: 10- and 11-year-olds
Content Area: Social studies

Technology: Laptops
Learning Environment: 1:1 laptops

The United States is often referred to as a "melting pot." That was true at one time, but today, the percentages of immigrants living in 67 other countries is far higher than in the U.S., where just 14.3 percent of the population is made up of immigrants. Why do people leave one country to live in another? What factors impact their choices about where to go? How do beliefs and behaviors of their cultures of origin influence their transitions into new lives?

Students in American education programs typically study immigration during the Colonial period when they are 10 to 11 years old. They learn about why people came to the New World between 1660 and 1775. This is a perfect opportunity for them to engage in an on-going project in which they learn about where their families came from originally, when and why. It also provides an opportunity to partner with students in one of the countries that has a much higher immigrant population than the U.S. in order to draw comparisons between the immigrant populations in each country. This is a timely topic for students to explore as nations around the world grapple with the impact of immigration.

In this example, students in an American school joined forces with students at a school in Singapore (where the immigrant population is nearly 43 percent) on a semester-long collaborative project. They began by developing an online survey each class member used to interview and capture responses from adult family members. They needed to gather data that could be dropped into a spreadsheet and then analyzed to compare immigration patterns between the families of the two classes. This required developing questions, testing them to be sure the results could be easily analyzed and rewriting questions as needed.

Once the survey was approved by teachers, each student interviewed an adult family member and entered responses into the survey that were then automatically added to a spreadsheet. Students then used an online tool to create a database of information about their families' origins – where they originally came from, when they moved, why they immigrated to a new country and if/how their cultures of origin still impact their lives. Students developed questions they wanted to ask about the data, then learned how to sort and filter their results. They next learned how to create charts and graphs to illustrate the answers to their questions. Their final results were published online and will be used as the foundation for continuation of the project next year.

In addition to offering opportunities for students to connect with counterparts in another country to conduct a timely study of the impact of immigration, teachers report that this project is an occasion for students to engage in iterative learning. Based on the premise that learning is an evolving process, iterative learning activities take place over time and are designed to encourage students to try out something, learn from mistakes and then try again. In this project, students develop, test and revise surveys and, once the data are collected, explore strategies for analyzing and reporting their results.

What is the connection to the Student Standards?

Knowledge Constructor – In the course of completing their study of immigration patterns, students build knowledge by actively exploring real-world issues and problems, developing ideas and theories, and pursuing answers and solutions.

Computational Thinker – As they work through this project, students collect data or identify relevant data sets, use digital tools to analyze them and represent data in various ways to facilitate problem-solving and decision-making.

Global Collaborator – This project offers opportunities for students to explore local and global issues using collaborative technologies to work with others to investigate solutions.

Scenarios for Ages 11-14

Scenario 1
Learning through Design Thinking

Eleven- to 14-year-old students use design thinking to work collaboratively to solve problems in their local community.

Age Level: 11- to 14-year-olds
Content Area: Science, social studies, mathematics
Learning Environment: Digital shop

Technology: Laptops, tablets, digital cameras, 3D design tools and printers, programmable robots and drones, open-source electronics platforms, an assortment of low- or no-tech materials including writeable desktops and hot glue guns.

Remember middle school shop class where students built birdhouses or fabricated their own hammers and chisels? Shop classes are not as common as they once were, for a variety of reasons. But the principal and teaching staff of one suburban middle school have committed to replacing traditional shop classes with digital shop classes.

You've undoubtedly heard references to transforming classroom learning by introducing design thinking into classrooms along with activities that help students develop empathy. These ideas are an important part of the foundation of digital shop, a program in which all students participate on a rotating basis (one week on, five weeks off) throughout the school year. What differentiates this class from similar STEM or STEAM programs is that every learning activity is tied directly to needs within the school's community. Design thinking provides a structure for giving students the skills they need to work collaboratively to solve problems. Focusing on needs within their own community helps students develop empathy as they strive to help people they know deal with real-world concerns.

What does this look like? First, students do not receive grades. This is to help students move beyond what the need to "pass" the class and shift their focus to what they need to do to find solutions to real problems that will benefit people they actually know. Next, students are able to work individually and/or in small groups. They may not come up with a good solution the first time around, but the idea is to allow them to learn from unsuccessful attempts – failure is an opportunity to learn, not an insurmountable obstacle. In addition to class time, students have access to online activities they may access at will, as part of after-school clubs, and some even come into the digital shop during their lunch time.

There are defined themes and special projects that tie back to students' learning in social studies, mathematics and science courses, but students have a lot of latitude when it comes to completing the activities. A sixth grade project focused on assistive technologies for a member of the school community with multiple sclerosis who had a double knee replacement. Mobility is a real issue for this person and the sixth graders explored design solutions to help her. A recent seventh grade project was a joint effort between students and a local medical center. The seventh graders helped medical staff identify and execute ways hospital stays can be made less scary for young children. Finally, eighth grade students are printing 3D prosthetics for a project that makes these devices available to children who need them.

What is the connection to the Student Standards?

Empowered Learner – An unexpected outcome of this program is the opportunity to help students learn to take more responsibility for their own learning. This is something many students need to learn how to do, and the projects are a good vehicle for this.

Digital Citizen – Because they are frequently working online and designing products, students have ample opportunities to practice positive, legal and ethical online behaviors. For example, they learn to protect their own privacy in the course of conducting research as well as the importance of adhering to copyright protections and respecting intellectual property as they create their designs.

Knowledge Constructor – In the course of conducting research related to design projects, students are afforded chances to find, analyze, curate and apply resources they discover, both online and offline.

Innovative Designer – Innovative design is the cornerstone of this approach to learning. Students have ample opportunities to employ design processes to identify and solve problems by creating new, useful or imaginative solutions.

Computational Thinker – Depending on the design challenge, students are encouraged to develop and employ strategies for understanding and solving problems in ways that leverage the power of technological methods to develop and test solutions.

Creative Communicator – Each project requires that individuals or teams be able to describe their design(s) and why this is an appropriate solution for the challenge.

Global Collaborator – Each design challenge is an opportunity for individuals or teams of students to enrich their learning by collaborating with others and working effectively in teams locally and globally.

Scenarios for Ages 11-14

Scenario 2
Making Algebra Accessible

Twelve- to 14-year-old students use an online tool to facilitate their mastery of complex algebraic concepts.

Age Level: 12- to 14-year-olds
Content Area: Mathematics (algebra)

Learning Environment: 1:1 classroom
Technology: Laptops, class set of 30 tablets

At the start of the 2015–16 school year, this small K–8 school launched pilot STEAM academies for students ages 12–14. Each age level focuses on a specific theme that offers a challenging, focused curriculum. Students from around the district were invited to enroll in the program, and all applicants were accepted. This is noteworthy because it means that students are there because it's where they want to be, not because they were included based on their academic skills. As a result, students are motivated, but represent a range of abilities.

Mathematics skills are foundational for many of the activities in the STEAM academies. The students study algebra to support the work they do in design and engineering classes. They regularly use a free online graphing calculator tool for functions, algebra, geometry, statistics, calculus and 3D math. This tool works online and is available in an app version for tablets and smartphones.

Their teacher reports that prior to having access to this tool, students labored over tasks like graphing linear equations or graphing on a coordinate plane. She reports that students were so focused on the mechanics of getting the data represented on paper, they missed the ultimate point of what they were doing and why. Now, thanks to the online tool, students are able to shift their attention from drawing a graph to what the graph represents. They are able to make predictions about ways changes in the data will impact the graph and then quickly test their guesses.

Students still learn how to create graphs by hand, but once they understand the basics for doing this, their use of technology removes barriers to learning. Students engage in more sophisticated activities because it's easier to get preliminary work out of the way. And even the less-skilled students are making enough progress in class to be able to apply their learning in engineering and design classes.

What is the connection to the Student Standards?

Computational Thinker – Use of the online graphing calculator enables students to use digital tools to analyze and represent data in various ways to facilitate problem-solving.

Scenarios for Ages 14-18

Scenario 1
Becoming Global Citizen Leaders

As part of their social studies and science coursework, high school students engage in long-term social action projects that address local and global issues. The culminating activity for these projects is a 3- to 5-minute video about each project.

Age Level: 14- to 18-year-olds
Content Areas: Language arts, social studies, science

Learning Environment: Classroom, computer lab, library/media center
Technology: Any device that can record video (digital camera, tablet, smartphone, etc.), laptops

Service learning that is grounded in either the social studies or science curriculum is a time-honored way for students to explore real-world issues and develop empathy and leadership skills by reaching out to help others. Over time, this idea has morphed from very short-term goals, such as a club-sponsored clothing drive, to projects that last one or two semesters. There are even programs where students are participating in multi-year social action projects. Students attending the high school featured here are transitioning from single to multi-year program commitments focused on local examples of global issues. The purpose of these activities is to encourage students to develop skills they need to become global citizen leaders. Broad project topics include: human rights, ethical issues, respect for law, the environment, the underprivileged, various disabilities, psycho-social issues, culture and heritage.

A critical piece of these projects is the underlying digital and communication skills students must acquire to be successful in implementing and sharing projects that have a global focus. Accurate research requires digital literacy. Communication with participants not readily available on campus necessitates online collaboration of one form or another. Project management must be facilitated through effective use of productivity tools. And the sharing of stories entails using various forms of social media to spread the word. For example, in the course of creating their 3- to 5-minute videos, in addition to learning how to point a camera to shoot video, students are learning how to develop ideas and organize their stories. They explore ways that scripting, acting and editing are used to communicate ideas and shape viewers' opinions.

For students who want to participate, the high school hosts an annual film festival that spotlights the best of the videos submitted. Only those videos related to the social actions projects are accepted. The festival is a community effort with active participation from: faculty who advise students as they develop and implement their social action projects and assist with making the videos; parents who support their children during the process of creating their videos and then attend the festival event; and the students themselves who spend countless hours working on their entries. Past topics for videos have included: the Syrian refugee crisis; special needs that impact students, including autism and Down syndrome; eating disorders; animal rights; nature preservation; and bullying.

What is the connection to the Student Standards?

Empowered Learner – Each student or team of students selects and pitches a topic for a social action project that will be the basis for a 3- to 5-minute video. Students are offered a great deal of autonomy in this learning process and also are encouraged to experience learning in formal and informal environments.

Digital Citizen – The study of media literacy throughout this activity provides a platform for students to learn responsible use of language, acting and editing when presenting a case for something or making a point.

Knowledge Constructor – Throughout this project, students explore real-world issues, pursuing answers or solutions. They are encouraged to plan and conduct effective research and evaluate the resources they find, both print and digital. They use the information they gather to build connections and draw conclusions.

Creative Communicator – Throughout this activity, students are creating an original work with the purpose of clearly communicating complex ideas. The final video presents content about their social projects in a manner designed to get their point across to parents, educators and fellow students.

Global Collaborator – Learning skills that will enable students to function as global citizens is one of the foundations of this project. This is embodied in the collaborative nature of the projects and opportunities to examine issues from multiple points of view as students explore local and global issues.

Scenarios for Ages 14-18

Scenario 2
Business and Ethics

High school students enrolled in a business management course as part of the International Baccalaureate Diploma Program (IBDP) apply what they are learning to complete a project about marketing.

Age Level: 16- to 18-year-olds
Content Areas: Business management, marketing
Learning Environment: 1:1 classroom

Technology: Laptops, tablets for checkout, students' personal devices

It is true that the IBDP program is rigorous, but within its framework, students are encouraged to thrive not just academically, but emotionally, ethically and physically. Civic responsibility is an important element in the IBDP program. Students are afforded many opportunities to develop skills in project management, ethics and empathy designed to ensure that they become responsible global citizens.

Given the current climate in many businesses around the world today, students enrolled in the business management course at one high school are encouraged to pay special attention to thoughtful, ethical business practices. One unit in the course focuses on marketing. As students learn about topics like marketing planning, sales forecasting, marketing research and e-commerce, they work in teams to apply their learning to development of a product or service that is designed to address a local or global issue. Ideas range from developing products to help deal with the global water crisis, to setting up micro-financing programs to help low-income people establish a small business, to organizing disaster relief for victims of natural disasters.

Once teams identify an idea for a product or service, they create a specific plan around marketing it. Related tasks include data collection and analysis for marketing research (proof of need for the product, target audience, price points), website design, and creation of a basic social media plan for product or service promotion. Teams collaborate online and offline to complete their work. Finally, they develop a report on their marketing plan that is delivered to the class and posted online.

What is the connection to the Student Standards?

Digital Citizen – Students consider ethical behavior as they use technology to complete the marketing project.

Knowledge Constructor – Students explore real-world issues, pursuing answers or solutions. They use the information they gather to build connections, draw conclusions and identify a product or service in response to an important global issue.

Innovative Designer – The point of this project is to use a process to identify and solve problems by creating new, useful or imaginative solutions in the form of a product or service. Use of technology is an integral part of the project.

Computational Thinker – As they develop a marketing plan, students collect data or identify relevant data sets, use digital tools to analyze them, and then represent data in various ways to facilitate problem-solving and decision-making.

Global Collaborator – In the course of completing this project, students explore local and global issues and use collaborative technologies to work with others to investigate solutions.

Age Band Articulation

ISTE developed age band articulations of the standards to support educators understanding of how they can be used with students of all ages and to provide relevance to teachers working with students of specific ages. These articulations can be used by classroom teachers to design age-appropriate learning activities targeted to the students they teach. Curriculum teams can use the articulations to develop a scope and sequence or to map curriculum for their school to ensure that students build necessary the foundation to take with them to their next level of schooling. Technology coaches and staff developers can design professional learning and support that is relevant to teachers no matter what age student they teach. Educator preparation programs can use these articulations with teacher candidates and to inform curriculum, and edtech resource developers can use the articulations to ensure their products meet the needs of their target student audience.

This section of the booklet includes articulations for ages 4–7, 8–11 and 12–14. For students ages 15 and older, the Student Standards themselves are appropriate.

Age Band Articulation: Ages 4-7

1. Empowered Learner

Students leverage technology to take an active role in choosing, achieving and demonstrating competency in their learning goals, informed by the learning sciences.

1.a.   With guidance from an educator, students consider and set personal learning goals and utilize appropriate technologies that will demonstrate knowledge and reflection of the process.

1.b.   With guidance from an educator, students learn about various technologies that can be used to connect to others or make their leaning environments personal and select resources from those available to enhance their learning.

1.c.   With guidance from an educator, students recognize performance feedback from digital tools, make adjustments based on that feedback and use age-appropriate technology to share learning.

1.d.   With guidance from an educator, students explore a variety of technologies that will help them in their learning and begin to demonstrate an understanding of how knowledge can be transferred between tools.

2. Digital Citizen

Students recognize the rights, responsibilities and opportunities of living, learning and working in an interconnected digital world, and they act in ways that are safe, legal and ethical.

2.a.   Students practice responsible use of technology through teacher-guided online activities and interactions to understand how the digital space impacts their life.

2.b.   With guidance from an educator, students understand how to be careful when using devices and how to be safe online, follow safety rules when using the internet and collaborate with others.

2.c.   With guidance from an educator, students learn about ownership and sharing of information, and how to respect the work of others.

2.d.   With guidance from an educator, students demonstrate an understanding that technology is all around them and the importance of keeping their information private.

3. Knowledge Constructor

Students critically curate a variety of resources using digital tools to construct knowledge, produce creative artifacts and make meaningful learning experiences for themselves and others.

3.a.   With guidance from an educator, students use digital tools and resources, contained within a classroom platform or otherwise provided by the teacher, to find information on topics of interest.

3.b.   With guidance from an educator, students become familiar with age-appropriate criteria for evaluating digital content.

3.c.   With guidance from an educator, students explore a variety of teacher-selected tools to organize information and make connections to their learning.

3.d.   With guidance from an educator, students explore real-world issues and problems and share their ideas about them with others.

4. Innovative Designer

Students use a variety of technologies within a design process to solve problems by creating new, useful or imaginative solutions.

4.a. With guidance from an educator, students ask questions, suggest solutions, test ideas to solve problems and share their learning.

4.b. Students use age-appropriate digital and non-digital tools to design something and are aware of the step-by-step process of designing.

4.c. Students use a design process to develop ideas or creations, and they test their design and redesign if necessary.

4.d. Students demonstrate perseverance when working to complete a challenging task.

5. Computational Thinker

Students develop and employ strategies for understanding and solving problems in ways that leverage the power of technological methods to develop and test solutions.

5.a. With guidance from an educator, students identify a problem and select appropriate technology tools to explore and find solutions.

5.b. With guidance from an educator, students analyze age-appropriate data and look for similarities in order to identify patterns and categories.

5.c. With guidance from an educator, students break a problem into parts and identify ways to solve the problem.

5.d. Students understand how technology is used to make a task easier or repeatable and can identify real-world examples.

6. Creative Communicator

Students communicate clearly and express themselves creatively for a variety of purposes using the platforms, tools, styles, formats and digital media appropriate to their goals.

6.a. With guidance from an educator, students choose different tools for creating something new or for communicating with others.

6.b. Students use digital tools to create original works.

6.c. With guidance from an educator, students share ideas in multiple ways – visual, audio, etc.

6.d. With guidance from an educator, students select technology to share their ideas with different people.

7. Global Collaborator

Students use digital tools to broaden their perspectives and enrich their learning by collaborating with others and working effectively in teams locally and globally.

7.a. With guidance from an educator, students use technology tools to work with friends and with people outside their neighborhood, city and beyond.

7.b. With guidance from an educator, students use technology to communicate with others and to look at problems from different perspectives.

7.c. With guidance from an educator, students take on different team roles and use age-appropriate technologies to complete projects.

7.d. With guidance from an educator, students use age-appropriate technologies to work together to understand problems and suggest solutions.

Age Band Articulation: Ages 8-11

1. Empowered Learner

Students leverage technology to take an active role in choosing, achieving and demonstrating competency in their learning goals, informed by the learning sciences.

1.a. Students develop learning goals in collaboration with an educator, select the technology tools to achieve them, and reflect on and revise the learning process as needed to achieve goals.

1.b. With the oversight and support of an educator, students build a network of experts and peers within school policy and customize their environments to enhance their learning.

1.c. Students seek from feedback from both people and features embedded in digital tools, and use age-appropriate technology to share learning.

1.d. Students explore age-appropriate technologies and begin to transfer their learning to different tools or learning environments.

2. Digital Citizen

Students recognize the rights, responsibilities and opportunities of living, learning and working in an interconnected digital world, and they act in ways that are safe, legal and ethical.

2.a. Students demonstrate an understanding of the role an online identity plays in the digital world and learn the permanence of their decisions when interacting online.

2.b. Students practice and encourage others in safe, legal and ethical behavior when using technology and interacting online, with guidance from an educator.

2.c. Students learn about, demonstrate and encourage respect for intellectual property with both print and digital media when using and sharing the work of others.

2.d. Students demonstrate an understanding of what personal data is, how to keep it private and how it might be shared online.

3. Knowledge Constructor

Students critically curate a variety of resources using digital tools to construct knowledge, produce creative artifacts and make meaningful learning experiences for themselves and others.

3.a. Students collaborate with a teacher to employ appropriate research techniques to locate digital resources that will help them in their learning process.

3.b. Students learn how to evaluate sources for accuracy, perspective, credibility and relevance.

3.c. Using a variety of strategies, students organize information and make meaningful connections between resources.

3.d. Students explore real-world problems and issues and collaborate with others to find answers or solutions.

4. Innovative Designer

Students use a variety of technologies within a design process to solve problems by creating new, useful or imaginative solutions.

4.a. Students explore and practice how a design process works to generate ideas, consider solutions, plan to solve a problem or create innovative products that are shared with others.
4.b. Students use digital and non-digital tools to plan and manage a design process.
4.c. Students engage in a cyclical design process to develop prototypes and reflect on the role that trial and error plays.
4.d. Students demonstrate perseverance when working with open-ended problems.

5. Computational Thinker

Students develop and employ strategies for understanding and solving problems in ways that leverage the power of technological methods to develop and test solutions.

5.a. Students explore or solve problems by selecting technology for data analysis, modeling and algorithmic thinking, with guidance from an educator.
5.b. Students select effective technology to represent data.
5.c. Students break down problems into smaller parts, identify key information and propose solutions.
5.d. Students understand and explore basic concepts related to automation, patterns and algorithmic thinking.

6. Creative Communicator

Students communicate clearly and express themselves creatively for a variety of purposes using the platforms, tools, styles, formats and digital media appropriate to their goals.

6.a. Students recognize and utilize the features and functions of a variety of creation or communication tools.
6.b. Student create original works and learn strategies for remixing or repurposing to create new artifacts.
6.c. Students create digital artifacts to communicate ideas visually and graphically.
6.d. Students learn about audience and consider their expected audience when creating digital artifacts and presentations.

7. Global Collaborator

Students use digital tools to broaden their perspectives and enrich their learning by collaborating with others and working effectively in teams locally and globally.

7.a. Students use digital tools to work with friends and people from different backgrounds or cultures.
7.b. Students use collaborative technologies to connect with others, including peers, experts and community members, to explore different points of view on various topics.
7.c. Students perform a variety of roles within a team using age-appropriate technology to complete a project or solve a problem.
7.d. Students work with others using collaborative technologies to explore local and global issues.

Age Band Articulation: Ages 12-14

1. Empowered Learner

Students leverage technology to take an active role in choosing, achieving and demonstrating competency in their learning goals, informed by the learning sciences.

1.a. Students articulate personal learning goals, select and manage appropriate technologies to achieve them, and reflect on their successes and areas of improvement in working toward their goals.

1.b. Students identify and develop online networks within school policy, and customize their learning environments in ways that support their learning, in collaboration with an educator.

1.c. Students actively seek performance feedback from people, including teachers, and from functionalities embedded in digital tools to improve their learning process, and they select technology to demonstrate their learning in a variety of ways.

1.d. Students are able to navigate a variety of technologies and transfer their knowledge and skills to learn how to use new technologies.

2. Digital Citizen

Students recognize the rights, responsibilities and opportunities of living, learning and working in an interconnected digital world, and they act in ways that are safe, legal and ethical.

2.d. Students manage their digital identities and reputations within school policy, including demonstrating an understanding of how digital actions are never fully erasable.

2.b. Students demonstrate and advocate for positive, safe, legal and ethical habits when using technology and when interacting with others online.

2.c. Students demonstrate and advocate for an understanding of intellectual property with both print and digital media – including copyright, permission and fair use – by creating a variety of media products that include appropriate citation and attribution elements.

2.d. Students demonstrate an understanding of what personal data is and how to keep it private and secure, including the awareness of terms such as encryption, HTTPS, password, cookies and computer viruses; they also understand the limitations of data management and how data-collection technologies work.

3. Knowledge Constructor

Students critically curate a variety of resources using digital tools to construct knowledge, produce creative artifacts and make meaningful learning experiences for themselves and others.

3.a. Students demonstrate and practice the ability to effectively use research strategies to locate appropriate digital resources in support of their learning.

3.b. Students practice and demonstrate the ability to evaluate resources for accuracy, perspective, credibility and relevance.

3.c. Students locate and collect resources from a variety of sources and organize assets into collections for a wide range of projects and purposes.

3.d. Students explore real-world issues and problems and actively pursue an understanding of them and solutions for them.

4. Innovative Designer

Students use a variety of technologies within a design process to solve problems by creating new, useful or imaginative solutions.

4.a. Students engage in a design process and employ it to generate ideas, create innovative products or solve authentic problems.

4.b. Students select and use digital tools to support a design process and expand their understanding to identify constraints and trade-offs and to weigh risks.

4.c. Students engage in a design process to develop, test and revise prototypes, embracing the cyclical process of trial and error and understanding problems or setbacks as potential opportunities for improvement.

4.d. Students demonstrate an ability to persevere and handle greater ambiguity as they work to solve open-ended problems.

5. Computational Thinker

Students develop and employ strategies for understanding and solving problems in ways that leverage the power of technological methods to develop and test solutions.

5.a. Students practice defining problems to solve by computing for data analysis, modeling or algorithmic thinking.

5.b. Students find or organize data and use technology to analyze and represent it to solve problems and make decisions.

5.c. Students break problems into component parts, identify key pieces and use that information to problem solve.

5.d. Students demonstrate an understanding of how automation works and use algorithmic thinking to design and automate solutions.

6. Creative Communicator

Students communicate clearly and express themselves creatively for a variety of purposes using the platforms, tools, styles, formats and digital media appropriate to their goals.

6.a. Students select appropriate platforms and tools to create, share and communicate their work effectively.

6.b. Students create original works or responsibly repurpose other digital resources into new creative works.

6.c. Students communicate complex ideas clearly using various digital tools to convey the concepts textually, visually, graphically, etc.

6.d. Students publish or present content designed for specific audiences and select platforms that will effectively convey their ideas to those audiences.

7. Global Collaborator

Students use digital tools to broaden their perspectives and enrich their learning by collaborating with others and working effectively in teams locally and globally.

7.a. Students use digital tools to interact with others to develop a richer understanding of different perspectives and cultures.

7.b. Students use collaborative technologies to connect with others, including peers, experts and community members, to learn about issues and problems or to gain broader perspective.

7.c. Students determine their role on a team to meet goals, based on their knowledge of technology and content, as well as personal preference.

7.d. Students select collaborative technologies and use them to work with others to investigate and develop solutions related to local and global issues.

Crosswalk

ISTE Standards for Students – 2016 to 2007

The following crosswalk compares the ISTE Standards for Students (2016) to the 2007 version. Use this crosswalk as a preliminary resource for supporting an adoption process to help identify gaps in your current policies.

The ISTE Standards for Students (2016) are included in the first column, with the corresponding standards and indicators from the Student Standards (2007), opposite.

ISTE Standards for Students (2016)

1. Empowered Learner
Students leverage technology to take an active role in choosing, achieving and demonstrating competency in their learning goals, informed by the learning sciences.

ISTE Standards for Students (2007)

a. Articulate and set personal learning goals, develop strategies leveraging technology to achieve them, and reflect on the learning process itself to improve learning outcomes.

5. Digital Citizenship
   b. Demonstrate a positive attitude toward using technology that supports collaboration, learning and productivity.
   c. Demonstrate personal responsibility for lifelong learning.

b. Build networks and customize their learning environments in ways that support the learning process.

2. Communication and Collaboration
   a. Interact, collaborate and publish with peers, experts or others employing a variety of digital environments and media.

c. Use technology to seek feedback that informs and improves their practice and to demonstrate their learning in a variety of ways.

5. Digital Citizenship
   b. Demonstrate a positive attitude toward using technology that supports collaboration, learning and productivity.

d. Understand the fundamental concepts of technology operations, demonstrate the ability to choose, use and troubleshoot current technologies, and are able to transfer their knowledge to explore emerging technologies.

6. Technology Operations and Concepts
   a. Understand and use technology systems.
   b. Select and use applications effectively and productively.
   c. Troubleshoot systems and applications.
   d. Transfer current knowledge to learning of new technologies.

2. Digital Citizen
Students recognize the rights, responsibilities and opportunities of living, learning and working in an interconnected digital world, and they act and model in ways that are safe, legal and ethical.

ISTE Standards for Students (2007)

a. Cultivate and manage their digital identity and reputation and are aware of the permanence of their actions in the digital world.

b. Engage in positive, safe, legal and ethical behavior when using technology, including social interactions online or when using networked devices.

5. Digital Citizenship
   d. Exhibit leadership for digital citizenship.

c. Demonstrate an understanding of and respect for the rights and obligations of using and sharing intellectual property.

5. Digital Citizenship
   a. Advocate and practice safe, legal and responsible use of information and technology.

d. Manage their personal data to maintain digital privacy and security and are aware of data-collection technology used to track their navigation online.

ISTE Standards for Students (2016)

3. Knowledge Constructor
Students critically curate a variety of resources using digital tools to construct knowledge, produce creative artifacts and make meaningful learning experiences for themselves and others.

a. Plan and employ effective research strategies to locate information and other resources for their intellectual or creative pursuits.

ISTE Standards for Students (2007)

3. Research and Information Fluency
  a. Plan strategies to guide inquiry.
  b. Locate, organize, analyze, evaluate, synthesize and ethically use information from a variety of sources and media.

b. Evaluate the accuracy, perspective, credibility and relevance of information, media, data or other resources.

3. Research and Information Fluency
  b. Locate, organize, analyze, evaluate, synthesize and ethically use information from a variety of sources and media.
  c. Evaluate and select information sources and digital tools based on the appropriateness to specific tasks.

c. Curate information from digital resources using a variety of tools and methods to create collections of artifacts that demonstrate meaningful connections or conclusions.

3. Research and Information Fluency
  c. Evaluate and select information sources and digital tools based on the appropriateness to specific tasks.

d. Build knowledge by actively exploring real-world issues and problems, developing ideas and theories, and pursuing answers and solutions.

4. Critical Thinking, Problem Solving and Decision Making
  d. Use multiple processes and diverse perspectives to explore alternative solutions.

4. Innovative Designer
Students use a variety of technologies within a design process to solve problems by creating new, useful or imaginative solutions.

ISTE Standards for Students (2007)

a. Know and use a deliberate design process for generating ideas, testing theories, creating innovative artifacts or solving authentic problems.

1. Creativity and Innovation
  a. Apply existing knowledge to generate new ideas, products or processes
4. Critical Thinking, Problem Solving and Decision Making
  a. Identify and define authentic problems and significant questions for investigation.
  d. Use multiple processes and diverse perspectives to explore alternative solutions.

b. Use digital tools to support a design process and expand their understanding to identify constraints and trade-offs and to weigh risks.

4. Critical Thinking, Problem Solving and Decision Making
  b. Plan and manage activities to develop a solution or complete a project.

c. Develop, test and refine prototypes as part of a cyclical design process.

4. Critical Thinking, Problem Solving and Decision Making
  d. Use multiple processes and diverse perspectives to explore alternative solutions.

d. Exhibit a tolerance for ambiguity, perseverance and the capacity to work with open-ended problems.

ISTE Standards for Students (2016)

5. Computational Thinker
Students develop and employ strategies for understanding and solving problems in ways that leverage the power of technological methods to develop and test solutions.

a. Formulate problem definitions suited for technology-assisted methods such as data analysis, abstract models and algorithmic thinking in exploring and finding solutions.

b. Collect data or identify relevant data sets, use digital tools to analyze them, and represent data in various ways to facilitate problem-solving and decision-making.

c. Break problems into component parts, extract key information, and develop descriptive models to understand complex systems or facilitate problem-solving.

d. Understand how automation works and use algorithmic thinking to develop a sequence of steps to create and test automated solutions.

ISTE Standards for Students (2007)

4. **Critical Thinking, Problem Solving and Decision Making**
   a. Identify and define authentic problems and significant questions for investigation.

1. **Creativity and Innovation**
   d. Identify trends and forecast possibilities.
3. **Research and Information Fluency**
   d. Process data and report results.
4. **Critical Thinking, Problem Solving and Decision Making**
   c. Collect and analyze data to identify solutions and/or make informed decisions.

4. **Critical Thinking, Problem Solving and Decision Making**
   d. Use multiple processes and diverse perspectives to explore alternative solutions.

6. Creative Communicator
Students communicate clearly and express themselves creatively for a variety of purposes using the platforms, tools, styles, formats and digital media appropriate to their goals.

a. Choose the appropriate platforms and tools for meeting the desired objectives of their creation or communication.

b. Create original works or responsibly repurpose or remix digital resources into new creations.

c. Communicate complex ideas clearly and effectively by creating or using a variety of digital objects such as visualizations, models or simulations.

d. Publish or present content that customizes the message and medium for their intended audiences.

ISTE Standards for Students (2007)

3. **Research and Information Fluency**
   c. Evaluate and select information sources and digital tools based on the appropriateness to specific tasks.

1. **Creativity and Innovation**
   a. Apply existing knowledge to generate new ideas, products or processes.
   b. Create original works as a means of personal or group expression.

1. **Creativity and Innovation**
   c. Use models and simulations to explore complex systems and issues.
2. **Communication and Collaboration**
   b. Communicate information and ideas effectively to multiple audiences using a variety of media and formats.

2. **Communication and Collaboration**
   a. Interact, collaborate and publish with peers, experts or others employing a variety of digital environments and media.
   b. Communicate information and ideas effectively to multiple audiences using a variety of media and formats.

ISTE Standards for Students (2016)

7. Global Collaborator
Students use digital tools to broaden their perspectives and enrich their learning by collaborating with others and working effectively in teams locally and globally.

a. Use digital tools to connect with learners from a variety of backgrounds and cultures, engaging with them in ways that broaden mutual understanding and learning.

b. Use collaborative technologies to work with others, including peers, experts or community members, to examine issues and problems from multiple viewpoints.

c. Contribute constructively to project teams, assuming various roles and responsibilities to work effectively toward a common goal.

d. Explore local and global issues and use collaborative technologies to work with others to investigate solutions.

ISTE Standards for Students (2007)

2. Communication and Collaboration
  a. Interact, collaborate and publish with peers, experts or others employing a variety of digital environments and media.
  c. Develop cultural understanding and global awareness by engaging with learners of other cultures.

2. Communication and Collaboration
  a. Interact, collaborate and publish with peers, experts or others employing a variety of digital environments and media.

2. Communication and Collaboration
  d. Contribute to project teams to produce original works or solve problems.

4. Critical Thinking, Problem Solving and Decision Making
  b. Plan and manage activities to develop a solution or complete a project.

2. Communication and Collaboration
  a. Interact, collaborate and publish with peers, experts or others employing a variety of digital environments and media.
  c. Develop cultural understanding and global awareness by engaging with learners of other cultures.

4. Critical Thinking, Problem Solving and Decision Making
  d. Use multiple processes and diverse perspectives to explore alternative solutions.

Essential Conditions

Necessary conditions to effectively leverage technology for learning

Shared Vision
Proactive leadership in developing a shared vision for educational technology among all education stakeholders, including teachers and support staff, school and district administrators, teacher educators, students, parents and the community.

Empowered Leaders
Stakeholders at every level empowered to be leaders in effecting change.

Implementation Planning
A systemic plan aligned with a shared vision for school effectiveness and student learning through the infusion of Information and Communication Technology (ICT) and digital learning resources.

Consistent and Adequate Funding
Ongoing funding to support technology infrastructure, personnel, digital resources and staff development.

Equitable Access
Robust and reliable access to current and emerging technologies and digital resources, with connectivity for all students, teachers, staff and school leaders.

Skilled Personnel
Educators, support staff and other leaders skilled in the selection and effective use of appropriate ICT resources.

Ongoing Professional Learning
Technology-related professional learning plans and opportunities with dedicated time to practice and share ideas.

Technical Support
Consistent and reliable assistance for maintaining, renewing and using ICT and digital learning resources.

Curriculum Framework
Content standards and related digital curriculum resources that are aligned with and support digital age learning and work.

Student-Centered Learning
Planning, teaching and assessment centered around the needs and abilities of students.

Assessment and Evaluation
Continuous assessment of teaching, learning and leadership and evaluation of the use of ICT and digital resources.

Engaged Communities
Partnerships and collaboration within communities to support and fund the use of ICT and digital learning resources.

Support Policies
Policies, financial plans, accountability measures and incentive structures to support the use of ICT and other digital resources for learning and in district school operations.

Supportive External Context
Policies and initiatives at the national, regional and local levels to support schools and teacher preparation programs in the effective implementation of technology for achieving technology as well as ICT standards.

Technology Scope and Sequence

The following K–12 Technology Scope and Sequence was developed by the educational technology faculty at Shorecrest Preparatory School (shorecrest.org). Shorecrest is a preschool through high school non-sectarian, co-ed, independent school in St. Petersburg, Florida.

Use this scope and sequence to identify prerequisite technology skills and recognize students' proficiency and progression across grade levels.

Key: ☐ Beginning (B) ☐ Developing (D) ☐ Secure (S)

Basic Operations & Concepts	K	1	2	3	4	5	6	7	8	9	10	11	12
Identify the basic components of the computer: monitor, keyboard, mouse, headphones, ports and printers.	B	D	S	S	S	S	S	S	S	S	S	S	S
Turn on/off a computer, laptop and/or hand-held device and log in.	B	B	D	D	S	S	S	S	S	S	S	S	S
Use a mouse or trackpad to manipulate shapes, icons; click on URLs, radio buttons, check boxes; use scroll bar.	B	B	D	D	D	S	S	S	S	S	S	S	S
Use desktop icons, windows and menus to open and close applications and documents; understand difference between closing and quitting applications.	B	B	B	B	B	D	D	S	S	S	S	S	S
Use shortcuts to operate the computer (i.e. Command-P, Command-C, Command-V).	B	B	B	D	D	D	D	S	S	S	S	S	S
Use gestures to navigate hand-held devices.	B	B	B	B	D	D	S	S	S	S	S	S	S
Use the print dialog box to select local printers and change settings (i.e. number of copies, color, paper size, orientation, scale, one-sided vs. two-sided).		B	B	B	B	B	D	D	S	S	S	S	S
Use basic troubleshooting steps to solve technical problems independently.			B	B	B	B	D	S	S	S	S	S	S
Apply prior technical knowledge and experiences to figure out how new technologies or applications work.		B	B	B	B	D	D	S	S	S	S	S	S
Manage and deploy software updates.						B	D	D	S	S	S	S	S

Logins/File Management	K	1	2	3	4	5	6	7	8	9	10	11	12
Use login credentials for access to network devices, accounts, servers, printers and cloud services.		B	B	B	D	D	S	S	S	S	S	S	S
Name documents with appropriate file names and understand where files are being saved.		B	B	B	B	D	D	D	S	S	S	S	S
Create, save, edit, copy and rename files and folders to organize documents and materials.		B	B	B	B	B	D	D	S	S	S	S	S
Delete files and folders; recover files and folders from the trash; empty trash.			B	B	B	B	D	D	S	S	S	S	S
Retrieve previous file revisions/access revision history for documents located in cloud services.				B	B	B	D	D	S	S	S	S	S
Download, upload, attach and zip files and folders via email or cloud services.				B	B	B	D	D	S	S	S	S	S
Use search tools to locate files and applications.		B	B	D	D	S	S	S	S	S	S	S	S
Can associate document extensions with appropriate file types.			B	B	B	D	D	S	S	S	S	S	S
Understand how cloud computing is different from using software applications.			B	B	D	D	D	S	S	S	S	S	S
Is able to upload/download/retrieve files to and from the cloud.			B	B	D	D	D	S	S	S	S	S	S

Key: ☐ Beginning (B) ☐ Developing (D) ☐ Secure (S)

Personal Data Management	K	1	2	3	4	5	6	7	8	9	10	11	12
Protect accounts by logging out of shared equipment.	B	B	B	D	D	D	D	S	S	S	S	S	S
Keep passwords confidential, and be proactive if they are compromised.	B	B	B	D	D	D	D	S	S	S	S	S	S
Use passcodes/passwords to secure individual devices.		B	B	D	D	S	S	S	S	S	S	S	S
Create robust passwords and effectively manage password privacy.		B	D	D	D	D	S	S	S	S	S	S	S
Find and adjust privacy settings.					B	B	D	D	D	S	S	S	S

Online Safety	K	1	2	3	4	5	6	7	8	9	10	11	12
Use technology independently and with peers responsibly, and make safe choices.		B	B	D	D	D	S	S	S	S	S	S	S
Understand how to be safe online and in a digital world.	B	B	B	B	B	D	D	D	D	D	D	S	S
Understand the importance of not sharing personal information online.	B	B	B	B	B	D	D	D	D	S	S	S	S
Understand how to practice safe internet searches.				B	B	B	D	D	D	D	D	S	S
Evaluate whether sources/websites are safe to conduct research.				B	B	B	D	D	D	D	D	S	S
Understand the positive and negative effects social media sites can have on one's life.				B	B	B	B	D	D	D	D	S	S

Digital Identity	K	1	2	3	4	5	6	7	8	9	10	11	12
Recognize how overuse of technology can impact one's mental, physical and emotional health.			B	B	B	B	D	D	D	D	D	D	D
Set appropriate profile pictures and other profile content across social media, web pages, blogs, etc.					B	B	B	B	B	B	D	D	S
Understand that digital content is permanent and cannot be deleted.				B	B	B	B	B	D	D	D	S	S
Build a positive digital footprint/reputation.				B	B	B	B	B	D	D	D	D	D
Recognize the difference between active and passive data collection when using the internet and social media sites.							B	B	D	D	D	D	D
Understand how browser settings such as cookies track personal information.							B	B	D	D	D	D	D

Keyboarding	K	1	2	3	4	5	6	7	8	9	10	11	12
Use keyboarding programs and games to assist in development of skills.	B	B	D	D	D	D	D	S	S	S	S	S	S
Use proper posture and ergonomics.	B	B	D	D	D	D	S	S	S	S	S	S	S
Locate and use letter and number keys with correct left and right hand placement (home row).	B	B	B	D	D	D	D	S	S	S	S	S	S
Locate and use correct finger/hand for space bar, return/enter and shift key.	B	B	D	D	D	S	S	S	S	S	S	S	S
Gain profiency and speed in touch-typing.	B	B	B	D	D	D	D	S	S	S	S	S	S
Learn to use special characters as needed (i.e. accents, tilda).			B	B	B	B	D	D	S	S	S	S	S

Key: ☐ Beginning (B) ☐ Developing (D) ☐ Secure (S)

Painting & Drawing Programs	K	1	2	3	4	5	6	7	8	9	10	11	12
Use basic drawing tools including pencil, paint brush, shape, line, undo, redo and eraser.	B	B	D	S	S	S	S	S	S	S	S	S	S
Use color palette/color wheel to change tool color.	B	D	S	S	S	S	S	S	S	S	S	S	S
Use selection tools to copy, paste, move and modify work.			B	D	D	D	D	S	S	S	S	S	S
Use text tool to add text features to artwork.	B	D	S	S	S	S	S	S	S	S	S	S	S
Use basic design principles (i.e. whitespace, color, balance, texture).						B	D	D	S	S	S	S	S

Communication & Collaboration Tools	K	1	2	3	4	5	6	7	8	9	10	11	12
Is polite and respectful in all communications and collaborations using technological tools, using appropriate language at all times.	B	B	D	D	D	S	S	S	S	S	S	S	S
Use email, messaging and other tools to share information and communicate ideas with others.			B	D	D	D	S	S	S	S	S	S	S
Compose and send an email.			B	D	D	D	S	S	S	S	S	S	S
Understand the difference between Reply Send, Reply All and Forward when responding to an email.			B	B	D	D	D	S	S	S	S	S	S
Understand the difference between CC (carbon copy) and BCC (blind carbon copy) and use them appropriately.						B	B	D	D	D	D	S	S
Attach a document or file to an email.					B	B	D	S	S	S	S	S	S
Use a course or learning management system to access class pages, class calendars, portfolios and grades.			B	D	D	D	S	S	S	S	S	S	S
Use features of a course or learning management system such as discussion forums, polls, wikis, dropbox, etc. to access and complete assignments.			B	D	D	D	S	S	S	S	S	S	S
Access calendar and student pages on school website as needed.			B	B	D	D	D	S	S	S	S	S	S
Use audience response tools and apps to participate in class discussions.	B	B	B	B	B	D	D	D	S	S	S	S	S
Set up, share and utilize collaborative workspaces, documents or other digital tools for asynchronous and synchronous collaboration.			B	D	D	D	D	S	S	S	S	S	S
Use synchronous collobaration tools such as video conferencing, interactive television and voice over IP to connect with others.	B	B	D	D	D	D	S	S	S	S	S	S	S
Use virtual world and gaming tools to work collaboratively toward common goals.		B	B	B	D	D	D	D	D	S	S	S	S
Use social media tools to connect, collaborate and share.				B	B	D	D	S	S	S	S	S	S
Use digital tools such as blogs, websites and social media to crowdsource, crowd fund and mobilize a community toward a goal.			B	B	B	B	B	D	D	D	D	S	S
Create and maintain a digital portfolio or collection of works related to one's learning.	B	B	D	D	D	D	D	D	D	S	S	S	S

Word Processing	K	1	2	3	4	5	6	7	8	9	10	11	12
Use a word processing application to write, edit, print and save assignments.	B	B	D	D	S	S	S	S	S	S	S	S	S
Use the menu/tool bar functions to format, edit and print a document.		B	D	D	D	D	D	S	S	S	S	S	S
Highlight, copy and paste text within a document or from an outside source.	B	B	D	D	S	S	S	S	S	S	S	S	S
Insert and resize images within a document.			B	D	D	D	S	S	S	S	S	S	S
Copy, paste and resize images found from oustide sources.			B	B	D	D	S	S	S	S	S	S	S
Use the menu/toolbar functions to format a paper using MLA, APA or other appropriate style.						B	B	B	D	S	S	S	S
Proofread and edit writing using built-in resources (i.e. dictionary, spell checker, thesaurus, grammar check).		B	B	D	D	D	D	S	S	S	S	S	S

Key: ☐ Beginning (B) ☐ Developing (D) ☐ Secure (S)

Problem-Solving & Computational Thinking	K	1	2	3	4	5	6	7	8	9	10	11	12
Use technology tools to represent solutions to problems in a variety of ways including text, sounds, pictures and numbers.	B	B	B	D	D	D	D	D	S	S	S	S	S
Use technology resources and tools to solve age-appropriate computing problems or for independent learning.	B	B	B	D	D	D	D	D	S	S	S	S	S
Define an algorithm as a sequence of instructions and use the basic steps of algorithmic thinking to solve problems and design solutions.	B	B	B	D	D	D	D	D	S	S	S	S	S
Use a block-based visual programming interface to build a game, tell a story or solve a problem.	B	B	B	B	B	D	D	D	S	S	S	S	S
Use 2D design tools to create prototypes, models and simulations to demonstrate solutions and ideas.	B	B	D	D	D	D	D	D	S	S	S	S	S
Use 3D design tools to create prototypes, models and simulations to demonstrate solutions and ideas.	B	B	B	B	B	B	D	D	D	D	D	S	S

Spreadsheets & Databases	K	1	2	3	4	5	6	7	8	9	10	11	12
Understand that spreadsheets, databases and other specialized data tools are used to collect, manage, analyze and visualize data.		B	B	B	D	D	D	S	S	S	S	S	S
Identify and explain terms and concepts related to spreadsheets (i.e. cell, column, row, values, labels, chart, graph).				B	B	B	D	D	S	S	S	S	S
Enter/edit data and text into a spreadsheet and format spreadsheet to accomodate data.				B	B	B	D	D	S	S	S	S	S
Calculate numerical equations using spreadsheet formulas and functions.							B	D	D	S	S	S	S
Designate the format of a cell to accomodate different kinds of text and numerical data.					B	B	D	D	S	S	S	S	S
Utilize spreadsheet data to create tables, charts and graphs.					B	B	D	D	S	S	S	S	S
Identify and explain terms and concepts related to database systems (i.e. field, set, subset, query, ordered, sorted).			B	B	B	D	D	D	S	S	S	S	S
Enter/edit data and/or text into a database and use queries to find information.				B	B	B	D	D	S	S	S	S	S
Use spreadsheets and databases to make predictions, solve problems and draw conclusions.						B	B	D	D	S	S	S	S

Multimedia & Presentation Tools	K	1	2	3	4	5	6	7	8	9	10	11	12
Use a digital camera, video camera or camera on a hand-held device to take pictures and videos.	B	B	D	D	S	S	S	S	S	S	S	S	S
Capture images that incorporate rules of photography.	B	B	B	D	D	D	D	S	S	S	S	S	S
Use photo- and video-editing tools to adjust images and add effects.	B	B	B	B	D	D	D	S	S	S	S	S	S
Save images in multiple formats.						B	B	D	D	S	S	S	S
Use recording and editing equipment to record, edit and publish audio.	B	B	B	B	D	D	D	S	S	S	S	S	S
Create, edit and format text, visuals and audio within a multimedia presentation.	B	B	B	D	D	D	S	S	S	S	S	S	S
Create a series of slides and organize them to present research or convey an idea.	B	B	D	D	D	D	S	S	S	S	S	S	S
Copy/paste or import graphics within a multimedia presentation. Be able to change their size and position on a slide.				B	B	D	D	S	S	S	S	S	S
Insert songs, videos or other media on slides.		B	B	B	D	D	D	S	S	S	S	S	S
Add a working hyperlink to a multimedia presentation.				B	B	D	D	D	S	S	S	S	S

Key: ☐ Beginning (B) ▨ Developing (D) ☐ Secure (S)

Internet Searching & Online Databases	K	1	2	3	4	5	6	7	8	9	10	11	12
Use refresh, forward and back buttons to navigate a web browser.	B	B	D	D	S	S	S	S	S	S	S	S	S
Use tab browsing to navigate multiple pages.	B	B	D	D	S	S	S	S	S	S	S	S	S
Create bookmarks and add frequently used sites to the bookmark bar.			B	B	D	D	D	S	S	S	S	S	S
Locate the URL of a website and make a distinction between the suffixes .org, .com, .edu, .net, .gov and international domains.	B	B	B	D	D	D	D	S	S	S	S	S	S
Use age-appropriate search engines to find information.	B	B	B	B	D	D	D	S	S	S	S	S	S
Use browser search tools and advanced search features to find information.		B	B	B	D	D	D	S	S	S	S	S	S
Use a browser's History feature to locate previously visited sites.		B	B	D	D	D	S	S	S	S	S	S	
Identify and use hyperlinks within web pages or documents.	B	B	D	D	S	S	S	S	S	S	S	S	S
Use digital tools or platforms to organize, display, annotate and/or share a curated collection.					B	B	B	D	D	D	D	S	S
Locate and add browser or other web apps or add-ons to customize learning.					B	B	D	D	S	S	S	S	S
Access online catalogs and databases for research.			B	B	B	B	D	D	D	D	S	S	S

Acceptable Use, Copyright & Plagiarism	K	1	2	3	4	5	6	7	8	9	10	11	12
Locate required citation information on web pages and other digital resources and cite in the appropriate style.		B	B	B	D	D	D	D	D	S	S	S	S
Use age-appropriate guidelines to evaluate websites and other resources for accuracy, perspective, credibility and relevance.		B	B	B	D	D	D	D	D	S	S	S	S
Transfer the information learned from online sources into your own words.		B	B	B	D	D	D	D	D	D	S	S	S
Understand all rules and guidelines in the school's Responsible Use Policy.	B	B	B	D	D	D	D	D	D	D	S	S	S
Understand Fair Use guidelines and their application to all forms of work.		B	B	B	B	D	D	D	D	S	S	S	

Organizational & Project Tools	K	1	2	3	4	5	6	7	8	9	10	11	12
Use a calendar, task manager or other tools to organize one's self as well as manage projects.			B	B	B	D	D	D	D	S	S	S	S
Use age-appropriate note-taking tools.	B	B	B	D	D	D	D	S	S	S	S	S	S
Use graphic organizers, brainstorming applications or other digital tools to gather and organize information.	B	B	D	D	D	D	S	S	S	S	S	S	S
Use digital tools to create timelines of people, historical events, etc. to organize information sequentially.			B	B	B	B	D	D	D	D	D	S	S

Development Team and Credits

Stakeholder Advisory Council

Chris Adams, Association of California School Administrators
Adam Bellow, eduClipper
Ron Canuel, Canadian Education Association
Richard Culatta, U.S. Department of Education (former) and State of Rhode Island (former)
S. Dallas Dance, Baltimore County Public Schools
Lori Gracey, Texas Computer Education Association
Cheryl Lemke, Metiri Group
Sylvia Martinez, author and independent consultant
Caitlin McLemore, The Harpeth Hall School
Helen Padgett, Arizona State University
Shawn Rubin, Highlander Institute
Mahmud Shihab, International College

Technical Working Group

Barry Bachenheimer, Pascack Valley Regional High School District
David Barr, Independent Education Management Professional
Alice Christie, education consultant and Arizona State University professor emerita
Richard Culatta, U.S. Department of Education (former) and State of Rhode Island (former)
Elizabeth M. Dalton, Dalton Education Services International
Kara Dawson, Unified Elementary Education, University of Florida
Laura Deisley, Reimagin:Ed and The Lovett School
Steve Hauk, Half Hollow Hills Central School District
Kathy Hayden, California State University, San Marcos
John Keller, Metropolitan School District of Warren Township
Kathryn Kennedy, Michigan Virtual University
Chrystalla Mouza, University of Delaware
Michelle Otstot, Copper Ridge Elementary School
Lisa Perez, Chicago Public Schools
William D. Simpson, Prince George's County Public Schools
Ben Smith, Red Lion Area School District
Andrew Wheelock, Erie 1 BOCES

Core Team

Anna Baralt, Shorecrest Preparatory School
Wendy Drexler, independent consultant
Jim Flanagan, ISTE
Mindy Frisbee, ISTE
LeeAnn Lindsey, Mary Lou Fulton Teachers College – Arizona State University
Yolanda Ramos, ISTE
Sarah Stoeckl, ISTE
Carolyn Sykora, ISTE

Content Development Team

Susan Brooks-Young, author (Introduction & Scenarios)
Emily Reed, editor
Julie Phillips Randles, copy editor